Enduring Words

FOR THE
TEACHER

Enduring Words
FOR THE
TEACHER

School Specialty
Publishing

School Specialty. **Publishing**

Anthology: Margaret Miller
Design: Zoë Murphy

This anthology © The Five Mile Press Pty Ltd

This edition published in the United States in 2006 by School Specialty
Publishing, a member of the School Specialty Family.

Library of Congress Cataloging-in-Publication Data is on file with the publisher.

Send all inquiries to:

School Specialty Publishing
8720 Orion Place
Colombus, OH 43240-2111

ISBN 0-7696-4755-3

Printed in China
1 2 3 4 5 6 7 8 9 FMP 09 08 07 06 05

www.SchoolSpecialtyPublishing.com

CONTENTS

PREFACE

There is nothing more admirable than to arrive at one's place of work each day with the intent to seek out the great potential in another person, young or old. A teacher does just this—devotes his or her life to others, helping them to know themselves, discover their worth, and cultivate the gifts they will give to the world. Teachers have the power to bring peace between races, religions, and cultures; to provide a foundation of knowledge and purpose to those who might otherwise turn to idleness, drugs, or violence; to nurture those who would be lost to loneliness and despair; and to open the world and all that it offers to those who may never have left their own neighborhoods.

This anthology recognizes and pays tribute to the invaluable contribution teachers have made to society. We hope that it will, in turn, inspire new teachers to continue the great tradition, improving the world generation by generation.

Curiosity

Never lose a holy curiosity.

Albert Einstein, 1879–1955
German-born American physicist

$\mathcal{T}$he whole art of teaching

is only the art of awakening

the natural curiosity of young minds

for the purpose of satisfying it afterwards.

Anatole France, 1844–1924
French writer, critic

Curiosity is a gift,

a capacity for pleasure in knowing,

which if you destroy, you make yourselves

cold and dull.

John Ruskin, 1819–1900
English art critic, philosopher, reformer

I keep six honest serving-men –

They taught me all I know;

Their names are What and Why and When

And How and Where and Who.

Rudyard Kipling, 1865–1936
Indian-born British poet, writer

It is important that students bring

a certain ragamuffin, barefoot irreverence

to their studies; they are not here

to hero-worship what is known

but to question it.

Jacob Bronowski, 1908–1974
Polish-born American writer, scientist

I find that a great part of the information I have acquired was by looking up something and finding something else on the way.

Franklin P. Adams, 1881–1960
American businessman

If I had influence

with the good fairy who is supposed to preside

over the christening of all children,

I should ask that her gift to each child in the world

would be a sense of wonder so indestructible

that it would last throughout life.

Rachel Carson, 1907–1964
American biologist, writer

We learn more by looking for the answer to a question and not finding it than we do from learning the answer itself.

Lloyd Alexander, b. 1924
American writer

*T*here are no foolish questions,

and no man becomes a fool

until he has stopped asking questions.

Charles Proteus Steinmetz, 1865–1923
German-born American engineer

*S*eize the moment of excited curiosity

on any subject to solve your doubts;

for if you let it pass, the desire may never return,

and you may remain in ignorance.

William Wirt, 1772–1834
American lawyer, poet

The important thing

is to not stop questioning.

Curiosity has its own reason for existing.

One cannot help but be in awe when one

contemplates the mysteries of eternity, of life,

of the marvelous structures of reality.

Albert Einstein, 1879–1955
German-born American physicist

*M*illions saw the apple fall,

but Newton asked why.

Bernard Baruch, 1870–1965
American financier, presidential adviser

*Those with
a lively sense of curiosity
learn something new
every day of their lives.*

———

Anonymous

A generous and elevated mind

is distinguished by nothing more certainly

than an eminent degree of curiosity.

Samuel Johnson, 1709–1784
English lexicographer, critic, writer

You can teach a student a lesson a day;

but if you can teach him to learn

by creating curiosity,

he will continue the learning process

as long as he lives.

Clay P. Bedford, 1903–1991
American writer

$\mathcal{D}$isinterested intellectual curiosity

is the lifeblood of real civilization.

George Macaulay Trevelyan, 1876–1962
British historian

For a man who cannot wonder

is but a pair of spectacles behind which

there are no eyes.

Thomas Carlyle, 1795–1881
Scottish historian, essayist, critic

*W*hoever retains

the natural curiosity of childhood

is never bored or dull.

———

Anonymous

$\mathcal{I}$ have no special talents.

I am only passionately curious.

Albert Einstein, 1879–1955
German-born American physicist

*T*he cure for boredom is curiosity.

There is no cure for curiosity.

Dorothy Parker, 1893–1967
American writer, poet, wit

Only the curious will learn,

and only the resolute

overcome the obstacles to learning.

The quest quotient has always excited me

more than the intelligence quotient.

Eugene S. Wilson, 1905–1981
Dean of Amherst College

What Makes a Good Teacher?

*W*hoever would be a teacher of men,

let him begin by teaching himself

before teaching others;

and let him teach by example

before teaching by word.

For he who teaches himself

and rectifies his own ways

is more deserving of respect and reverence

than he who would teach others

and rectify their ways.

Kahlil Gibran, 1883–1931
Lebanese poet, artist, mystic

I am not a teacher

but an awakener.

Robert Frost, 1874–1963
American poet

I like a teacher who gives you

something to take home to think about

besides homework.

Lily Tomlin, b. 1939
American actress, comedian

*T*he best teacher is the one

who suggests rather than dogmatizes

and inspires his listener with

the wish to teach himself.

Edward Bulwer-Lytton, 1803–1873
English writer, politician

$\mathcal{G}$ood teaching
is one-fourth preparation
and three-fourths theater.

Gail Godwin, b. 1937
American writer, journalist, educator

A teacher affects eternity:

He can never tell where his influence stops.

Henry Adams, 1838–1918
American historian, journalist

$\mathcal{T}$he most effective teacher
will always be biased,
for the chief force in teaching
is confidence and enthusiasm.

Joyce Cary, 1888–1957
Irish novelist

*E*ach day, I learn more than I teach;

I learn that half knowledge of another's life

leads to false judgment;

I learn that there is a surprising kinship

in human nature;

I learn that it is a wise father who knows his son;

I learn that what we expect we get;

I learn that there's more good than evil in this world;

that age is a question of spirit;

that youth is the best of life

no matter how numerous its years;

I learn how much there is to learn.

Virginia K. Church, b. 1937
American educator, writer

$\mathcal{D}$on't try to fix the students; fix ourselves first.

The good teacher makes the poor student good

and the good student superior.

When our students fail,

we, as teachers, too, have failed.

Marva Collins, b. 1936
American educator, social activist

What you teach your children

is what you really believe in.

Cathy Warner Weatherford, b. 1951
American educator

The task of the excellent teacher is to stimulate 'apparently ordinary' people to unusual effort. The tough problem is not in identifying winners; it is in making winners out of ordinary people.

K. Patricia Cross, b. 1926
American educator

*H*e that teaches us

anything which we knew not before

is undoubtedly to be revered as a master.

Samuel Johnson, 1709–1784
English lexicographer, critic, essayist

A master can tell you

what he expects of you.

A teacher, though,

awakens your own expectations.

Patricia Neal, b. 1926
American actress

*T*ell me, and I'll forget.

Show me, and I may not remember.

Involve me, and I'll understand.

———————————
Native American saying

*I*t is the supreme art of the teacher

to awaken joy in creative expression

and knowledge.

Albert Einstein, 1879–1955
German-born American physicist

*O*ne good teacher in a lifetime

may sometimes change a delinquent

into a solid citizen.

Philip Wylie, 1902–1971
American writer

A teacher should have

maximum authority

and minimal power.

Thomas Szaz, b. 1920
American psychiatrist

What nobler employment,

or more valuable to the state,

than that of the man who instructs

the rising generation.

Cicero, 106–43 BC
Roman statesman, writer

*T*eachers are expected to reach
unattainable goals with inadequate tools.
The miracle is that at times they accomplish
this impossible task.

Haim G. Ginott, 1922–1973
American child psychologist

A good teacher is like a candle

which consumes itself

to light the way for others.

———
Unknown

*O*ne looks back

with appreciation to the brilliant teachers

but with gratitude to those

who touched our human feelings.

The curriculum is so much necessary raw material,

but warmth is the vital element for the

growing plant and for the soul of the child.

Carl Jung, 1875–1961
Swiss psychologist

$\mathscr{A}$ man should first
direct himself in the way he should go.
Only then should he instruct others.

Buddha, c. 500 BC
Indian philosopher, founder of Buddhism

The teacher who is indeed wise

does not bid you

to enter the house of his wisdom

but rather leads you

to the threshold of your mind.

Kahlil Gibran, 1883–1931
Lebanese poet, artist, mystic

The best teachers

teach from the heart,

not from the book.

Unknown

*W*hy am I a teacher?

Because I'm good at it!

I choose it!

Ramona Greschel, b. 1939
American educator

*W*hat the teacher *is*, is more important
than what he teaches.

Karl Menninger, 1893–1990
American psychiatrist

*T*he role of the teacher remains
the highest calling of a free people.
To the teacher, America entrusts her
most precious resource, her children,
and asks that they be prepared,
in all their glorious diversity,
to face the rigors of individual participation
in a democratic society.

Shirley Hufstedler, b. 1925
American government official

*G*ood teachers are costly,

but bad teachers cost more.

———

Unknown

$\mathcal{T}$he secret of teaching

is to appear to have known all your life

what you just learned this morning.

———
Unknown

*G*ood teaching

is more a giving of right questions

than a giving of right answers.

Josef Albers, 1888–1976
German-born American art teacher

*A*merica's future will be determined

by the home and the school.

The child becomes largely what it is taught;

hence, we must watch what we teach

and how we live before it.

Jane Addams, 1860–1935
American social reformer, writer

The true teacher defends his pupils

against his own personal influence.

He inspires self-distrust.

He guides their eyes from himself

to the spirit that quickens him.

He will have no disciple.

Amos Bronson Alcott, 1799–1888
American educator, reformer

We expect teachers to handle teenage pregnancy, substance abuse, and the failings of the family. Then, we expect them to educate our children.

John Sculley, b. 1939
American computer software exucutive

The mediocre teacher tells.

The good teacher explains.

The superior teacher demonstrates.

The great teacher inspires.

William Arthur Ward, 1921–1997
American author, pastor, teacher

To teach is to learn.

Japanese proverb

*A*ny teacher can take a child to the classroom,

but not every teacher can make him learn.

He will not work joyously unless he feels

that liberty is his, whether he is busy or at rest;

he must feel the flush of victory and

the heart-sinking of disappointment before he

takes with a will the tasks distasteful to him

and resolves to dance his way bravely through

a dull routine of textbooks.

Helen Keller, 1880–1968
American writer, lecturer

Spoon feeding in the long run

teaches us nothing

but the shape of the spoon.

E. M. Forster, 1879–1970
English writer, essayist, critic

*T*eaching was the hardest work

I had ever done, and it remains

the hardest work I have done to date.

Ann Willis Richards, b. 1933
American Governor of Texas

$\mathcal{D}$on't set your wit

against a child.

Jonathan Swift, 1667–1745
Irish poet, essayist, satirist, cleric

Tapping Into Potential

Love not what you are

but what you may become.

Miguel de Cervantes, 1547–1616
Spanish writer

If we did all the things

we are capable of doing,

we would truly astound ourselves.

Thomas Edison, 1847–1931
American inventor

$\mathcal{W}$e should say to each [child]:

do you know what you are?

You are a marvel. You are unique ….

You may become a Shakespeare,

a Michelangelo, a Beethoven.

You have the capacity for anything.

Pablo Casals, 1876–1973
Spanish cellist, conductor, composer

$\mathcal{E}$very individual human
being born on this earth
has the capacity to become
a unique and special person
unlike any who has ever existed before
or will ever exist again.

Elisabeth Kübler Ross, 1926–2004
American psychiatrist, writer

If someone listens

or stretches out a hand

or whispers a word of encouragement

or attempts to understand a lonely person,

extraordinary things begin to happen.

Loretta Firzaris, b. 1920
American educator, writer

I have tried to write the best I can;

sometimes I have good luck

and write better than I can.

Ernest Hemingway, 1898–1961
American writer

*M*an's most important task is to

give birth to himself, to become

what he potentially is.

Eric Fromm, 1900–1980
German-born American psychologist, philosopher

*T*reat people as if they were

what they ought to be,

and you can help them become

what they are capable of becoming.

Johann Wolfgang von Goethe, 1749–1832
German poet, writer, scientist

*F*ree the child's potential,

and you will transform

him into the world.

Maria Montessori, 1870–1952
Italian educator, physician

$\mathcal{D}$on't let the best you have done so far

be the standard for the rest of your life.

Gustavus F. Swift, 1839–1903
American business manager

We must always change,

renew, rejuvenate;

otherwise, we harden.

Johann Wolfgang von Goethe, 1749–1832
German poet, writer, scientist

To be what we are

and to be what we are capable of becoming

is the only end in life.

Robert Louis Stevenson, 1850–1894
Scottish author, poet

I not only use all the brains I have but all I can borrow.

Woodrow Wilson, 1856–1925
President of the United States of America

Compared to what we ought to be,

we are only half-awake.

We are making use of only a small part

of our physical and mental resources.

Stating the thing broadly,

the human individual thus

lives far within his limits.

He possesses power of various sorts

which he habitually fails to use.

William James, 1842–1910
American psychologist, philosopher

$\mathcal{T}$he mind is an iceberg –

it floats with only

one-seventh of its bulk

above water.

Sigmund Freud, 1856–1939
Austrian founder of psychoanalysis

The educator must believe in the potential power of his pupil, and he must employ all his art in seeking to bring his pupil to experience this power.

Alfred Adler, 1870–1937
Austrian psychiatrist, psychologist

The great law of culture is:

Let each become all that he was

created capable of being.

Thomas Carlyle, 1795–1881
Scottish essayist, historian, critic

The creation of a thousand forests

is in one acorn.

Ralph Waldo Emerson, 1803–1882
American poet, essayist, teacher

In everyone

there is something precious,

found in no one else;

so honor each man

for what is hidden within him –

for what he has

and none of his fellows.

Hasidic saying

$\mathcal{T}$here's only one corner of the universe

you can be certain of improving

and that's your own self.

Aldous Huxley, 1894–1963
English writer

When I stand before God

at the end of my life,

I would hope that I would not

have a single bit of talent left

and could say,

'I used everything you gave me.'

Erma Bombeck, b. 1927
American writer, humorist

I do the very best I know how –

the very best I can;

and I mean to keep on doing it

until the end.

Abraham Lincoln, 1809–1865
President of the United States of America

$\mathcal{M}$y business

is not to remake myself

but make the absolute best

of what God made me.

Robert Browning, 1812–1899
English poet, playwright

The Importance of Imagination

$\mathcal{K}$nowledge is limited.

Imagination encircles the whole world.

Albert Einstein, 1879–1955
German-born American physicist

*I*magination is the beginning of creation.

You imagine what you desire,

you will what you imagine,

and at last you create what you will.

George Bernard Shaw, 1856–1950
Irish dramatist, essayist, critic

Creativity is so delicate a flower

that praise tends to make it bloom

while discouragement often nips it in the bud.

Any of us will put out more and better ideas

if our efforts are appreciated.

Alex F. Osborn, 1888–1966
American advertising director, writer

*T*hrow your dreams into space like a kite,

and you do not know what they will bring back:

a new life, a new friend, a new love,

a new country.

Anaïs Nin, 1903–1977
French novelist

*W*ithout leaps of imagination or dreaming,

we lose the excitement of possibilities.

Dreaming, after all, is a form of planning.

Gloria Steinem, b. 1934
American feminist, writer

*A*ll the things we achieve

are things we have first of all imagined.

David Malouf, b. 1934
Australian writer

To accomplish great things,

we must not only act but also dream,

not only plan but also believe.

Anatole France, 1844–1924
French writer

In every real man

a child is hidden

who wants to play.

Friedrich Nietzche, 1844–1900
German philosopher

*N*o matter how old you get,
if you can keep the desire to be creative,
you're keeping the man-child alive.

John Cassavetes, 1929–1988
American film director

*I*magination

is more important

than knowledge.

Albert Einstein, 1879–1955
German-born American physicist

*W*hat is now proved

was once only imagined.

William Blake, 1757–1827
English poet, artist, mystic

Imagination finds a road

to the realm of the gods,

and there man can glimpse

that which is to be

after the soul's liberation from

the world of substance.

Kahlil Gibran, 1883–1931
Lebanese poet, artist, mystic

*I*magination, industry, and intelligence –

the three I's – are indispensable to the actress;

but of these three, the greatest is,

without any doubt, imagination.

Ellen Terry, 1848–1928
English actress

$\mathcal{T}$he world is but the canvas

to our imagination.

Henry David Thoreau, 1817–1862
American essayist, poet

Imagination

is the highest kite

one can fly.

Lauren Bacall, b. 1924
American actress

*A*rt is an essential reminder
of what it is in life that lasts,
of why one lives.
Art communicates, celebrates,
mourns, and remembers.
What else in our lives can do this?

Bella Lewitzky, 1916–2004
American dancer, choreographer

Dreams

are the touchstones

of our character.

Henry David Thoreau, 1817–1862
American poet, essayist, teacher

$\mathscr{T}$here are no rules of architecture

for a castle in the clouds.

G.K. Chesterton, 1874–1936
English critic, novelist, poet

If you have built castles in the air,

your work need not be lost;

that is where they should be.

Now put the foundations under them.

Henry David Thoreau, 1817–1862
American poet, essayist, teacher

*W*hen I examine myself
and my methods of thought,
I come to the conclusion
that the gift of fantasy has meant
more to me than my talent
for absorbing positive knowledge.

Albert Einstein, 1879–1955
German-born American physicist

$\mathcal{S}$ome men see things as they are

and say, 'Why?'

I dream of things that never were

and say, 'Why not?'

George Bernard Shaw, 1856–1950
Irish dramatist, essayist, critic

Imagination
is the eye of the soul.

Joseph Joubert, 1754–1824
French writer, moralist

Go confidently

in the direction of your dreams!

Live the life you've imagined.

Henry David Thoreau, 1817–1862
American poet, essayist, teacher

*T*he future belongs

to those who believe

in the beauty of their dreams.

Eleanor Roosevelt, 1884–1962
First Lady of the United States of America

Our imagination

is the only limit

to what we can hope to

have in the future.

Charles F. Kettering, 1876–1958
American engineer, inventor

Reflections on Education

What we want to see

is the child in pursuit of knowledge

not knowledge

in pursuit of the child.

George Bernard Shaw, 1856–1950
Irish dramatist, essayist, critic

$\mathcal{N}$o one has yet realized

the wealth of sympathy,

the kindness and generosity

hidden in the soul of a child.

The effort of every true education

should be to unlock that treasure.

Emma Goldman, 1869–1940
American feminist, social activist

Education

is the transmission

of civilization.

Will Durant, 1885–1981
American philosopher, writer

The first idea that the child must acquire,

in order to be actively disciplined,

is that of the difference between good and evil;

and the task of the educator lies in seeing

that the child does not confound good

with immobility and evil with activity.

Our aim is to discipline for activity,

for work, for good – not for immobility,

not for passivity, not for obedience.

Maria Montessori, 1870–1952
Italian-born educator, physician

$\mathcal{E}$ducation should consist
of a series of enchantments,
each raising the individual
to a higher level of awareness,
understanding, and kinship
with all living things.

Unknown

Education makes a people

easy to lead but difficult to drive,

easy to govern but impossible to enslave.

Peter Brougham, 1778–1868
British politician

The purpose of learning is growth,

and our minds, unlike our bodies,

can continue growing

as we continue to live.

Mortimer Adler, 1902–2001
American philosopher, writer

The most important function

of education at any level

is to develop the personality of the individual

and the significance of his life

to himself and to others.

Grayson Kirk, 1903–1997
American educator

*E*ducation is not the filling of a pail

But the lighting of a fire.

William Butler Yeats, 1865–1939
Irish poet, mystic

$\mathcal{T}$he important thing is

not so much that every child should be taught

as that every child should be given

the wish to learn.

John Lubbock, 1834–1914
English banker

The whole purpose of education

is to turn mirrors into windows.

Sydney J. Harris, 1917–1986
American journalist

$\mathcal{E}$ducation is

the most powerful weapon

which you can use

to change the world.

Nelson Mandela, b. 1918
President of South Africa

The direction in which

education starts a man

will determine his future.

Plato, c. 429–347 BC
Greek philosopher

*E*ducation should be

gentle and stern,

not cold and lax.

Joseph Joubert, 1754–1824
French writer, moralist

If a nation expects

to be ignorant and free,

in a state of civilization,

it expects what never was

and will never be.

Thomas Jefferson, 1743–1826
President of the United States of America

*I*t is in fact a part of

the function of education

to help us escape,

not from our own time –

for we are bound by that –

but from the intellectual

and emotional limitations

of our time.

T. S. Eliot, 1888–1965
American-born poet, critic

$\mathcal{N}$ext in importance

to freedom and justice

is popular education, without which

neither freedom nor justice

can be permanently maintained.

James A. Garfield, 1831–1881
President of the United States of America

*The object of education
is to prepare the young
to educate themselves
throughout their lives.*

Robert M. Hutchins, 1899–1977
American educational reformer

*E*ducation is more than a luxury;

it is a responsibility

that society owes to itself.

Robin Cook, 1946–2005
British politician

*I*ntelligence plus character –

that is the goal of true education.

Martin Luther King, Jr., 1929–1968
American civil rights activist, minister

*E*ducation is a succession of eye-openers,

each involving the repudiation of

some previously held belief.

George Bernard Shaw, 1856–1950
British dramatist, essayist, critic

The job of an educator
is to teach students to see
the vitality in themselves.

Joseph Campbell, 1904–1987
American professor, writer

It is the mark of an educated mind

to be able to entertain a thought

without accepting it.

Aristotle, 384–322 BC
Greek philosopher

*T*he object of teaching a child

is to enable him to get along

without his teacher.

Elbert Hubbard, 1856–1915
American editor, writer

*P*erhaps the most valuable result of all education

is the ability to make yourself do

the thing you have to do, when it ought to be done,

whether you like it or not.

It is the first lesson that ought to be learned;

and however early a man's training begins,

it is probably the last lesson

that he learns thoroughly.

Thomas H. Huxley, 1825–1895
English scientist

*L*earning should be a joy

and full of excitement.

It is life's greatest adventure;

it is an illustrated excursion

into the minds of noble and learned men,

not a conducted tour through a jail.

Taylor Caldwell, 1900–1985
American writer

$\mathcal{T}$he primary purpose

of a liberal education

is to make one's mind a pleasant place

in which to spend one's leisure.

Sydney J. Harris, 1911–1986
American journalist

I can read Shakespeare and the Bible

and I can shoot dice.

That's what I call a liberal education.

Tallulah Bankhead, 1903–1968
American actress

That is what education is:

You suddenly understand something

you've understood all your life

but in a new way.

Doris Lessing, b. 1919
British writer

*E*ducation

is the best provision

for old age.

Aristotle, 384–322 BC
Greek philosopher

*E*ducation is the ability to

listen to almost anything

without losing your temper

or your self-confidence.

Robert Frost, 1874–1963
American poet

A child uneducated

is a child lost.

John F. Kennedy, 1917–1963
President of the United States of America

To make your children

capable of honesty

is the beginning of education.

John Ruskin, 1819–1900
English art critic, philosopher, reformer

*L*earning makes a man

fit company for himself.

Thomas Fuller, 1608–1661
English churchman, historian

*E*ducation is an admirable thing,

but it is well to remember from time to time

that nothing that is worth knowing

can be taught.

Oscar Wilde, 1854–1900
Irish poet, dramatist, writer, wit

*H*eadmasters

have powers at their disposal

with which Prime Ministers

have never yet been invested.

Sir Winston Churchill, 1874–1965
British Prime Minister, statesman, writer

When you educate a man,

you educate an individual;

when you educate a woman,

you educate a family.

Charles D. McIver, 1860–1906
American educator

$\mathcal{T}$he art of teaching

is the art of assisting discovery.

Mark Van Doren, 1894–1972
American poet, critic

$\mathcal{T}$he one object of education

is to have a man in the condition of

continually asking questions.

Bishop Mandell Creighton, 1843–1901
English historian

*T*o live for a time

close to great minds

is the best kind

of education.

John Buchan, 1875–1940
Scottish writer, lawyer, politician

$\mathcal{T}$he supreme end of education

is expert discernment in all things –

the power to tell the good from the bad,

the genuine from the counterfeit,

and to prefer the good and genuine

to the bad and counterfeit.

Samuel Johnson, 1709–1784
English lexicographer, critic, essayist

The roots of education are bitter,

but the fruit is sweet.

Aristotle, 384–322BC
Greek philosopher

*R*eading maketh a full man,

conference a ready man,

and writing an exact man.

Sir Francis Bacon, 1561–1626
English philosopher, essayist

The Power of the Mind

A stand can be made

against the invasion of an army;

no stand can be made

against the invasion of an idea.

Victor Hugo, 1802–1885
French poet, writer

The universe is transformation.

Our life is what our thoughts make it.

Marcus Aurelius, 121–180 AD
Roman emperor, philosopher

*E*very revolution

was once a thought

in one man's mind.

Ralph Waldo Emerson, 1803–1882
American poet, essayist, teacher

*W*hat was once thought

can never be unthought.

Friedrich Durrenmatt, 1921–1990
Swiss writer

*K*nowledge and understanding

are life's faithful companions

who will never be untrue to you.

For knowledge is your crown

and understanding your staff;

and when they are with you,

you can possess no greater treasures.

Kahlil Gibran, 1883–1931
Lebanese poet, artist, mystic

*A*ll that we are

is the result of what we have thought;

it is founded on our thoughts;

it is made up of our thoughts.

If a man speaks or acts with a pure thought,

happiness follows him

like a shadow that never leaves him.

Buddha, c. 500 BC
Indian philosopher, founder of Buddhism

If a man

empties his purse into his head,

no one can take it from him.

Benjamin Franklin, 1706–1790
American statesman, scientist

$\mathcal{T}$he mind of man

is capable of anything –

because everything is in it,

all the past as well as the future.

Joseph Conrad, 1857–1924
Polish-born English writer

A little knowledge that acts
is worth infinitely more
than knowledge that is idle.

Kahlil Gibran, 1883–1931
Lebanese poet, artist, mystic

*L*earning is a treasure

that will follow its owner everywhere.

Chinese proverb

*T*he beginning of knowledge

is the discovery of something

we do not understand.

Frank Herbert, 1920–1986
American science-fiction writer

A man

is what he thinks about

all day long.

Ralph Waldo Emerson, 1803–1882
American poet, essayist, teacher

When house and land are gone and spent

Then Learning is most excellent.

Samuel Foote, 1720–1777
English actor, dramatist, wit

$\mathcal{K}$nowledge is power itself.

Francis Bacon, 1561–1626
English philosopher, essayist

With our thoughts,

we make the world.

Buddha, c. 500 BC
Indian religious teacher, founder of Buddhism

$\mathscr{G}$reater than the tread of mighty armies

is an idea whose time has come.

Victor Hugo, 1802–1885
French poet, writer

*O*ne man who

has a mind and knows it

can always beat ten men

who haven't and don't.

George Bernard Shaw, 1856–1950
Irish dramatist, essayist, critic

Remember, Failure Isn't Permanent

*T*here is no failure

except in not trying.

Elbert Hubbard, 1856–1915
American editor, writer

*S*ay not that she did well or ill,

Only 'She did her best.'

Dina Maria Craik, 1826–1887
English novelist, poet

We learn wisdom from failure

much more than success.

We often discover what we *will* do

by finding out what we will *not* do.

Samuel Smiles, 1812–1904
Scottish writer, social reformer

*W*hen I was a young man,

I observed that

nine out of ten things I did

were failures.

I didn't want to be a failure,

so I did ten times more work.

George Bernard Shaw, 1856–1950
Irish dramatist, essayist, critic

Whenever I have found that I have blundered

or that my work has been imperfect,

and when I have been contemptuously criticized, …

it has been my greatest comfort to say

hundreds of times to myself that

I have worked as hard and as well as I could,

and no man can do more than this.

Charles Darwin, 1809–1882
British scientist

If at first you don't succeed,

you're running about average.

Margaret H. Alderson, b.1959
American journalist

*Y*ou must never conclude,

even though everything goes wrong,

that you cannot succeed.

Even at the worst, there is a way out,

a hidden secret

that can turn failure into success

and despair into happiness.

No situation is so dark

that there is not a ray of light.

***

Norman Vincent Peale, 1898–1993
American writer, minister

*I*f you can't make a mistake,

you can't make anything.

Marva Collins, b. 1936
American educator, social activist

A lot of successful people are risk-takers.

Unless you're willing to do that – to have a go,

fail miserably, and have another go –

success won't happen.

Phillip Adams, b.1939
Australian writer, radio broadcaster

And remember,

we all stumble,

every one of us.

That's why it's a comfort

to go hand in hand.

Emily Kimbrough, 1899–1989
American writer

$\mathcal{T}$here is only one real failure in life that is possible,

and that is not to be true to the best one knows.

Frederic Farrer, 1831–1903
English clergyman, writer

*N*othing in the world

can take the place of persistence.

Talent will not; nothing is more common

than unsuccessful men with talent.

Genius will not; unrewarded genius

is almost a proverb.

Education will not; the world is full

of educated failures.

Persistence and determination alone

are omnipotent.

Calvin Coolidge, 1872–1933
President of the United States of America

If you have made mistakes, ... there is

always another chance for you .... You may have

a fresh start at any moment you choose,

for this thing we call 'failure'

is not the falling down

but the staying down.

Mary Pickford, 1893–1979
American actress

Some of the best lessons we ever learn,

we learn from our mistakes and failures.

The error of the past is the

success and wisdom of the future.

Tyron Edwards, 1861–1941
American theologian

When we begin to take our failures non-seriously,

it means we are ceasing to be afraid of them.

It is of immense importance

to learn to laugh at ourselves.

Katherine Mansfield, 1888–1923
New Zealand short story writer

A Successful Career

*T*he best career advice to the young is:

Find out what you like doing best

and get someone to pay you for it.

Katharine Whitehorn, b. 1926
English newspaper columnist

*N*ever turn down a job

because you think it's too small;

you don't know where it could lead.

Julia Morgan, 1872–1957
American architect

*I*n order that people

must be happy in their work,

these three things are needed:

They must be fit for it;

they must not do too much of it;

and they must have a sense

of success in it.

John Ruskin, 1819–1900
English art critic, philosopher, reformer

$\mathcal{T}$o love what you do

and feel that it matters –

what could be more fun?

Katherine Graham, b. 1918
American newspaper publisher

*T*o my mind,

the best investment a young man

starting out in business could possibly make

is to give all his time, all his energies,

to work – just plain hard work.

Charles M. Schwab, 1862–1939
American industrialist

Flipping burgers is not beneath your dignity.

Your grandparents had

a different word for burger-flipping.

They called it opportunity.

Bill Gates, b. 1955
American computer software magnate

Often the difference

between a successful person and a failure

is not that one has better abilities or ideas

but the courage one has to bet on one's ideas —

to take a calculated risk — and to act.

Maxwell Maltz, 1899–1975
American surgeon, motivational writer

The men I have seen succeed

have always been cheerful and hopeful,

who went about their business

with a smile on their faces and took all

the changes and chances of this life

like a man.

Charles Kingsley, 1819–1875
English writer, poet, clergyman

*B*elieve in the best, think your best,

study your best, have a goal for the best,

never be satisfied with less than your best,

try your best, and in the long run

things will turn out for the best.

Henry Ford, 1863–1947
American automobile manufacturer

*A*ll successful people have a goal.

No one can get anywhere

unless he knows where he wants to go

and what he wants to do or be.

Norman Vincent Peale, 1898–1993
American writer, minister

*S*uccess is to be measured
not so much by the position
one has reached in life as by
the obstacles one has overcome
while trying to succeed.

Booker T. Washington, 1856–1915
American teacher, writer, speaker

$\mathcal{L}$aziness may appear attractive,

but work gives satisfaction.

Anne Frank, 1929–1945
Dutch schoolgirl, diarist

$\mathcal{P}$eople who are

unable to motivate themselves

must be content with mediocrity

no matter how impressive

their other talents.

Andrew Carnegie, 1835–1919
American industrialist, philanthropist

$\mathcal{N}$ever look down to test the ground

before taking your next step;

only he who keeps

his eye fixed on the far horizon

will find his right road.

Dag Hammarskjöld, 1905–1961
Swedish statesman, Secretary-General of the UN

*T*he first thing to do in life

is to do with purpose

what one proposes to do.

Pablo Casals, 1876–1973
Spanish cellist, conductor, composer

The only place

where success comes before work

is in a dictionary.

Vidal Sassoon, b. 1928
Enlish innovative hairstylist

If you want to succeed,

you should strike out on new paths

rather than travel the worn paths

of accepted success.

John D. Rockefeller, 1839–1937
American oil millionaire, philanthropist

$\mathcal{D}$o your work with all your heart

and you will succeed –

there's so little competition.

<hr>

Elbert Hubbard, 1856–1915
American editor, writer

My formula for success?

Rise early,

work late,

strike oil.

J. Paul Getty, 1892–1976
American oil magnate

A Lifetime of Learning

I am learning all the time.

The tombstone will be my diploma.

Eartha Kitt, b. 1927
American singer

*A*nyone who stops learning is old,

whether at twenty or eighty.

Henry Ford, 1863–1947
American automobile manufacturer

I am always ready to learn

although I do not always like

being taught.

Sir Winston Churchill, 1874–1965
British Prime Minister, statesman, writer

*E*ducation is a progressive

discovery of our ignorance.

Will Durant, 1885–1981
American author, historian

*Y*ou have learned something.

That always feels at first

as if you had lost something.

H.G. Wells, 1866–1946
British writer

$\mathcal{I}$ am defeated, and know it,

if I meet any human being from whom

I am unable to learn anything.

George Herbert Palmer, 1842–1933
American educator

*W*hat one knows is, in youth,

of little moment.

They know enough

who know how to learn.

Henry Adams, 1838–1918
American historian, novelist

Every act of conscious learning

requires a willingness to suffer

an injury to one's self-esteem.

That is why young children,

before they are aware

of their self-importance,

learn so easily.

Thomas Szas, b. 1920
American psychiatrist

*W*hat is important is to keep learning,

to enjoy the challenge,

and to tolerate ambiguity.

In the end, there are no certain answers.

———————

Martina Homer
President of Radcliffe College

Learning without thought is labor lost;
thought without learning is perilous.

Confucius, 551–479 BC
Chinese philosopher

I don't think much

of a man who is not wiser today

than he was yesterday.

Abraham Lincoln, 1809–1865
President of the United States of America

*R*ead not to contradict and confute,

nor to believe and take for granted,

but to weigh and consider.

Sir Francis Bacon, 1561–1626
English philosopher, essayist

*S*it down before fact

as a little child,

be prepared to give up

every conceived notion,

follow humbly wherever

and whatever abysses nature leads,

or you will learn nothing.

Thomas H. Huxley, 1825–1895
British scientist

$\mathcal{L}$earning is like rowing upstream:

Not to advance is to drop back.

———————

Chinese proverb

*B*ooks are the quietest

and most constant of friends;

they are the most accessible

and wisest of counselors

and the most patient of teachers.

Charles W. Eliot, 1834–1926
American educator

Words to Ponder

*B*reathe as if it's your last breath.

Touch as if you will remember the feel forever.

Kiss as though you will never kiss again.

Laugh as if it's the best sound.

Be as close to friends as you possibly can.

Live like it's your last day.

Love as if your heart has never been broken.

Don't follow the crowds;

be yourself, unique in every way.

Don't test your life for it's the one you chose.

Make it count forever.

Liz C.
Student aged 15

$\mathcal{A}$nd now here is my secret, a very simple secret:

It is only with the heart that one can see rightly;

what is essential is invisible to the eye.

Antoine de Saint-Exupery, 1900–1944
French novelist, aviator

The secret of happiness is this:

Let your interests be as wide as possible,

and let your reactions

to things and persons that interest you

be as far as possible friendly

rather than hostile.

Bertrand Russell, 1872–1970
English philosopher, mathematician

$\mathcal{T}$here can be no keener revelation

of a society's soul

than the way in which

it treats its children.

Nelson Mandela, b. 1918
President of South Africa

$\mathcal{M}$ ankind has become so much one family
that we cannot ensure our own prosperity
except by ensuring that of everyone else.
If you wish to be happy yourself,
you must resign yourself to seeing
others also happy.

Bertrand Russell, 1872–1970
English philosopher, mathematician

*W*e don't receive wisdom;

we must discover it for ourselves

after a journey

that no one can take for us.

Marcel Proust, 1871–1922
French writer, critic

When you arise in the morning,

give thanks for the morning light.

Give thanks for your life and strength.

Give thanks for your food.

And give thanks for the joy of living.

And if perchance you see no reason

for giving thanks,

rest assured the fault is in yourself.

Native American saying

$\mathcal{T}$o be content, look backward

on those who possess less than yourself

not forward to those who possess more.

Benjamin Franklin, 1706–1790
American statesman, scientist

*K*eep away from people

who try to belittle your ambitions.

Small people always do that,

but the really great

make you feel that you, too,

can become great.

Mark Twain, 1835–1910
American writer

$\mathcal{O}$ur problem is that we make the mistake

of comparing ourselves with other people.

You are not inferior or superior to any human being....

You do not determine your success by comparing yourself

to others; rather you determine your success by comparing

your accomplishments to your abilities. You are 'number one'

when you do the best you can with what you have, every day.

Zig Siglar, b. 1926
American motivational writer

You gain strength, courage, and confidence

by every experience in which

you really stop to look fear in the face.

You must do the thing you cannot do.

Eleanor Roosevelt, 1884–1962
First Lady of the United States of America

$\mathcal{W}$hen we do the best we can,

we never know what miracle

is wrought in our life

or the life of another.

Helen Keller, 1880–1968
American writer, lecturer

What is success?

To laugh often and much.

To win the respect of intelligent people

and the affection of children.

To earn the appreciation of honest critics

and endure the betrayal of false friends.

To appreciate beauty. To find the best in others.

To leave the world a bit better, whether by a healthy child,

a garden patch, or a redeemed social condition.

To know even one life breathed easier because you have lived.

This is to have succeeded.

Ralph Waldo Emerson, 1803–1882
American poet, essayist, teacher

Good sense travels on well-worn paths;

genius never.

Cesar Lombroso, 1836–1909
Italian founder of criminology

*E*ach person

has a basic decency and goodness.

If he listens to it and acts on it,

he is giving a great deal

of what the world needs most.

It is not complicated, but it takes courage.

It takes courage for a person

to listen to his own goodness

and act on it.

Pablo Casals, 1876–1973
Spanish cellist, conductor, composer

If a man does not keep pace

with his companions,

perhaps it is because

he hears a different drummer.

Let him step to the music which he hears

however measured or far away.

Henry David Thoreau, 1817–1862
American essayist, poet

You have to accept

whatever comes along,

and the only important thing

is that you meet it

with the best you have to give.

Eleanor Roosevelt, 1884–1962
First Lady of the United States of America

*E*xpect trouble as an inevitable part of life,

and when it comes, hold your head high,

look it squarely in the eye, and say,

'I will be bigger than you. You cannot defeat me.'

Then, repeat to yourself

the most comforting words of all,

'This too will pass.'

Ann Landers, 1918–2002
American advice columnist

To believe your own thoughts,

to believe that what is true for you

in your private heart

is true for all men –

that is genius.

Ralph Waldo Emerson, 1803–1882
American poet, essayist, teacher

A loving person lives in a loving world.

A hostile person lives in a hostile world.

Everyone you meet is your mirror.

Ken Keyes, Jr., 1921–1995
Personal growth leader, peace advocate